Independence

By Robert B. Winn

Preface

A house divided against itself cannot stand.

Abraham Lincoln

And if a house be divided against itself, that house cannot stand.

Mark 3:25

But he, knowing their thoughts, said unto them, Every kingdom divided against itself is brought to desolation, and a house divided against a house faileth.

Luke 11:17

Foreword

Two men met at Weehawken, New Jersey, on July 11, 1804. Both were prominent political party leaders of their time, members of opposing parties. After their meeting, the political careers of both were essentially over. Alexander Hamilton, the former Secretary of the Treasury and founder of America's first political party, the Federalist Party, was mortally wounded and only lived part of another day. The man who shot him, Aaron Burr, the Vice-President of the United States, was wanted in two states for murder. Burr had been elevated to the position of Vice-President by the Republican-Democrat Party because of his expertise in party organization.

Of the two men, Aaron Burr was more like the party politicians of today. He and Hamilton were unfortunate to live in a time when party politicians were settling party disputes with dueling pistols instead of with microphones. Politicians of today would try to spread their contention to their political followers and let them fight it out.

Chapter 1

In 1642 Charles I, King of England, declared war on his own Parliament. Charles did not see himself as an unreasonable king, but Parliament had taxed his patience. In the ensuing bloody civil war, the armies of the king were defeated by the armies of Parliament under Oliver Cromwell. The king was captured, sentenced to death for treason, and executed by beheading.

Parliament abolished the office of king forever, and England was declared to be a commonwealth and free state. Oliver Cromwell served as head of state with the title of Lord Protector of England until his death.

The death of Cromwell left Parliament with a problem they had not prepared to resolve. After an unsuccessful attempt to elevate Cromwell's son to the position of Lord Protector and several months of political confusion, Parliament requested that Charles, the son of Charles I, return to England from the European continent, where he had been living in exile, and become king. Charles graciously consented.

Charles II was not a good king. He had acquired some bad habits during his exile on the European continent. He was indolent, self-indulgent, and immoral. He did not have some of the good qualities of his father, Charles I; devotion to duty, courage, religious faith, and devotion to family and friends. But he had seen something his father had not seen until his last day on earth. A king could be deposed and executed.

Consequently, Charles II was more adapted to getting along with Parliament than his father had been. Still, there were some things that a king needed to impose. While a disagreement that included war might be understandable to a king, "regicide" was not. The "regicides" had to receive the just punishment for their crime. So the thirteen "regicides" who had sat on the High Court and voted for the execution of Charles I were hanged and drawn and quartered. The bodies of the great Lord Protector Cromwell and some of his subordinates were dug up, hung in shrouds, and then buried in a common pit.

Parliament could understand how Charles felt. The Parliament that had warred against Charles I had by now been mostly replaced by pro-royalty men. Regicide was bad, kings were necessary, and as long as Charles II was amenable to Parliament, Parliament would sustain the king. As long as the king did not declare war on Parliament the way his father had done, everything would be fine.

But Charles II had seen the days of glory of his grandfather, James I, and his father Charles I, two unpopular kings who had nevertheless imposed their will. His own position of weakness seemed like subservience to a political body that was supposed to be subject to him. There had to be a way to weaken Parliament.

Charles II found a way. The answer to his dilemma was political parties.

Chapter 2

Charles II was unfortunate to reign at a time when England was beset by one disaster after another. The first of these was the great plague of London, in which a large portion of the population of London expired from the bubonic plague. Charles II moved his royal court out of London into the countryside during this great disaster, leaving the battle against the plague to lesser officials, who buried the dead in huge mass graves dug in the middle of the city. They also imposed other measures, such as killing of all dogs and cats, which scientific minds of the day believed might be spreading the disease. This added an increase in the number of rats and other rodents in the city to the discomforts already being experienced, but, at least, the citizens could be certain that cats and dogs were not spreading the plague.

No sooner did the plague subside than the city of London caught on fire and, for the most part, burned to the ground.

These misfortunes did not provide Charles II with a favorable economic and political climate for increasing the power of royalty. Charles II was induced into accepting direct bribes from his cousin, Louis XIV of France, in return for helping France with a war against the Dutch and avoiding war with France, the natural enemy of England. It was during these political difficulties that Charles' attention was drawn to two disruptive factions in Parliament which called each other by the derisive names of Whigs and Tories. Whigs was short for Whiggamores, a troublesome group of Scottish separatists. Tories were an infamous band of Irish highwaymen. Whigs in Parliament tended to be nobility and wealthy merchants. Tories tended to be clergy and country gentry. The main question dividing Whigs and Tories concerned the "divine right of kings", as it applied to James, the brother of Charles II and the person likely to succeed him as king, since Charles II had no legitimate children. Tories supported the divine right of kings. Charles saw it to his immediate advantage to align himself with the Tories, not just because of his brother, but also because of his cousin, Louis XIV. An alliance with Tories would help Charles avoid the war with France that many Whigs wanted to see happen. Whigs questioned the divine right of kings and did not want to see James, an avowed Catholic, ascend to the throne of England.

For a weak and troubled king, the decisions of Charles II have an inordinate effect on governments of today. It was not just his decision to execute the judges who had sentenced his father to death that affected English speaking governments after his time. Even more influential over government today was his decision to select the ministers of his government from a specific party. This was so successful at weakening Parliament that it was written into English law during the reign of Queen Anne, the niece of Charles II.

If Charles II had been a bad king, his successor, James II, was a horrible one. With regard to Parliament, James was more like his father than his brother, and this elevated the Whigs into power fairly rapidly. James' daughter Mary, the wife of William of Orange of the Netherlands, decided to depose her father and arrived in England with an army. Without support from the English people, James II elected to flee to France, leaving his Protestant daughter and her Protestant husband as rulers of England. William, as King of England, went through Tory ministers and

Whig ministers as the majority changed back and forth in Parliament, finally ending with Whigs, which were members of the party he wanted. With the deaths, first of Mary and later of William after their successful reign, Mary's sister Anne became queen.

Queen Anne was a high Tory. She replaced most of William's Whig ministers with Tories, but the Whigs held a majority in Parliament. By the end of Anne's reign, the ministers were once again Whigs, and a law had been written that the monarch was required to appoint the ministers of government from the party which held a majority in Parliament. This was the official beginning of the two-party corruption that has dominated English speaking governments since that time.

Chapter 3

Despite seventeen pregnancies, Queen Anne died without any heirs to the throne. The Stuarts, the royal family of England, were really putting divine right of kings to the test. Not only had they put together two queens in succession, but now they were completely out of people, except for the little brother of the two queens. However, he had been raised as a Catholic in France, so he was not divine enough to become king of England. The Whigs started calling him The Pretender. It was at this critical juncture that the Whigs unaccountably lost their majority in Parliament. When Queen Anne suddenly died, there was no monarch to replace the Whig ministers still running the government. So as the majority party Tories tried to get James the Pretender enthroned, the Whigs went to Germany and located Queen Anne's closest living Protestant relative, a man named George living in Hanover, and declared him king of England.

George the First may have had a limited understanding of the English language, but he had no trouble discerning which side of his bread the butter was on. The Tories were the minority party for the next fifty years, as the Whigs had their way in government, becoming so corrupt that eventually the people of England had enough of them and voted them out of office.

The English people were on their third George, the great-grandson of the first one, when the Whigs were voted out, and the Tories came back into power amid promises of reform and honest government. The problem with reform and honest government when a political party is in power is that it can be very expensive, and any expenses incurred by a party in power are customarily paid for from public revenues. That is just the way political parties do things. So who should pay for the cost of reform and honest government in England?

Well, one reliable source of public revenues for the British empire was their colonies scattered around the world. Of these, one of the most profitable in the mid-eighteenth century was the American colonies, an established source of revenues for the English government. All that needed to be done was to increase taxes on the American colonies until reform and honest government were accomplished in England. What could possibly go wrong?

So Parliament immediately levied several new taxes on the American colonists, the Stamp Act, the tea tax, the Townshend Acts, etc., etc. Job done.

However, the American colonists trashed the Stamp Act offices, threw a shipload of tea into Boston harbor, declared independence from England, and defeated the British military in a war of revolution; all over some taxes that were minute compared to the taxes that American political parties have imposed on Americans of today.

Chapter 4

The two-party system in England that had resulted in a war of independence in America was a manifestation of a concept that was thought of as essential to European politics, balance of power. Balance of power was an idea that arose from the continual wars that European monarchs waged against each other. The premise was that no one nation should possess sufficient power to subjugate the rest. In practical terms, the people who put this idea into effect were the people who controlled European wealth, the bankers of Europe. If they thought that one nation was becoming too powerful in a war, they would build up the military of the weaker nation, prolong the war, and make money in the process from military contracts, often from both sides of the conflict. Since European monarchs were all related to each other by thinning blood, it was all in the family. War was a family game. Common people were thought of as existing to serve the state. It was the task of royalty to determine which nations would fight each other.

Once American independence was achieved, the prevailing idea in America was that the people of America were the government, and the councils of government existed to serve the people. This idea was particularly adapted to the American colonies, even when they were under British rule, because of the unity of the people at local level. Although there were political parties in the colonial assemblies, they pertained to England more than to the colonies, and once the Revolutionary War started, Tories in America were Americans who still supported England because the Tory Party in England had started the war. During the war and for a considerable time afterward, the goal of Americans was to establish a partyless government, a government in which the sovereignty of the nation belonged to the people, not to a king, and not to any privileged group.

With this in mind, Americans wrote the Articles of Confederation, establishing a national government that was too weak to solve most of the problems that arose. Accordingly, delegates from the states met in Philadelphia in 1787 to draft a new Constitution. There was some discussion at the convention of the idea of partyless government, which all of the delegates agreed was a good goal in drafting a Constitution. In the end, they agreed to make no mention of parties in the new Constitution. The preamble to the Constitution shows the concept of government that the framers had in mind, a united people who governed themselves by common consent, the powers of government dependent on the consent of the governed.

Ironically, it was over the question of adoption of the Constitution that the first great political division appeared in the United States, those for adoption being called Federalists, and those opposed being called Anti-Federalists. The arguments of the Federalists prevailed. The Constitution was ratified, and George Washington, who had presided over the Constitutional Convention, was elected the first President of the United States of America, with John Adams as Vice-President.

As his Secretary of Treasury, President Washington chose Alexander Hamilton, one of the leaders of the Federalist movement, and as his Secretary of State, Thomas Jefferson, who had been in France when the Constitution was written and adopted. These were the two men largely responsible for the system of two-party corruption that controls the United

States today. In a series of events reminiscent of the coronation of Charles II, two political parties started by Hamilton and Jefferson dominated the election of 1800. Independent voters, the voters created by the writing of the Constitution of the United States, have been prevented from being elected to public office since that time by party control of elections. The idea of partyless government, like the idea of abolishing the office of king in England, existed only briefly in the history of government before it was extinguished. However, there was enough independence in existence during the period between the writing of the Declaration of Independence and the election of 1800 that a Constitution was written that has lasted more than two hundred years.

Both of the first two Presidents spoke out against the formation of political parties. In his Farewell Address, President Washington set forth his ideas about the effect political parties would have on a purely elective government such as the one the people of the United States had started. Historians of today seem to take the position that Washington was secretly a member of the Federalist Party started by Alexander Hamilton and was insincere about what he said concerning political parties. Where they get that idea, I do not know. It is difficult for me to imagine a way to predict more closely what would happen to the freedoms established in America if political parties came to be supported by the people.

George Washington's comments about political parties are largely ignored today.

> "They serve to organize faction, to give it an artificial and extraordinary force, to put in the place of the delegated will of the nation the will of a party, often a small but artful and enterprising minority of the community, and according to the alternate triumphs of different parties to make the public administration the mirror of the ill-concerted and incongruous projects of faction, rather than the organ of consistent and wholesome plans digested by common councils and modified by mutual interests.

> "However combinations or associations of the above description may now and then answer popular ends, they are likely, in the course of time and things, to become

potent engines, by which cunning, ambitious, and unprincipled men will be enabled to subvert the power of the people, and to usurp for themselves the reins of government , destroying afterwards the very engines which have lifted them to unjust domination.

"Towards the preservation of your government and the permanency of your present happy state, it is requisite, not only that you steadily discountenance irregular oppositions to its acknowledged authority, but also that you resist with care the spirit of innovation upon its principles, however specious the pretexts. One method of assault may be to effect, in the forms of the Constitution, alterations which will impair the energy of the system, and thus to undermine what cannot be directly overthrown. In all the changes to which you may be invited, remember that time and habit are at least as necessary to fix the true character of governments as of other human institutions; that facility in changes, upon the credit of mere hypothesis and opinion, exposes to perpetual change, from the endless variety of hypothesis and opinion; and remember, especially, that for the efficient management of your common interests, in a country so extensive as ours, a government of as much vigor as is consistent with the perfect security of liberty is distributed and adjusted, its surest guardian. It is, indeed, little else than a name, where the government is too feeble to withstand the enterprises of faction, to confine each member of the society within the limits prescribed by the laws, and to maintain all in the secure and tranquil enjoyment of the rights of person and property.

"I have already intimated to you the danger of parties in the State, with particular reference to the founding of them on geographical discriminations. Let me now take a more comprehensive view, and warn you in the most solemn manner against the baneful effects of the spirit of party generally.

"This spirit, unfortunately, is inseparable from our nature, having its root in the strongest passions of the human mind. It exists under different shapes in all governments, more or less stifled, controlled, or repressed; but in those of the popular form, it is seen in its greatest rankness and is truly their worst enemy.

"The alternate domination of one faction over another, sharpened by the spirit of revenge, natural to party dissension, which in different ages and countries has perpetrated the most horrid enormities, is itself a frightful despotism. But this leads at length to a more formal and permanent despotism. The disorders and miseries which result gradually incline the minds of men to seek security and repose in the absolute power of an individual; and sooner or later the chief of some prevailing faction, more able or fortunate than his competitors, turns this disposition to the purposes of his own elevation, on the ruins of public liberty.

"Without looking forward to an extremity of this kind (which nevertheless ought not to be entirely out of sight), the common and continual mischiefs of the spirit of party are sufficient to make it the interest and duty of a wise people to discourage and restrain it.

"It serves always to distract the public councils and enfeeble the public administration. It agitates the community with ill-founded jealousies and false alarms, kindles the animosity of one part against another, foments occasionally riot and insurrection. It opens the door to foreign influence and corruption, which finds a facilitated access to the government itself through the channels of party passions. Thus the policy and will of one country are subjected to the policy and will of another.

"There is an opinion that parties in free countries are useful checks upon the administration of the government and serve to keep alive the spirit of liberty. This within certain limits is probably true; and in governments of a monarchical cast, patriotism may look with indulgence, if not with favor, upon the spirit of party. But in those of the popular character, in governments purely elective, it is a spirit not to be encouraged." (Farewell Address, 1796)

One of Washington's purposes in giving this advice was to warn against something that had been taking place within his own administration, a contention between Secretary of Treasury Alexander Hamilton and Secretary of State Thomas Jefferson. Hamilton had aligned himself with New England merchants and manufacturers and sought to advance their interests. As a result, his followers took upon themselves the characteristics of the Whig Party of England, which from its beginning had been comprised of nobility and wealthy merchants. The Whig Party of England had been less than enthusiastic in its support of the war with the American colonists. Hamilton wanted to have a strong alliance with England based on

Whig Party principles. Hamilton's followers called themselves Federalists and did not really consider themselves to be an organized political party until the election of 1800, when Thomas Jefferson and James Madison started the Republican-Democrat Party in opposition to the Federalists.

The Tory Party of England had caused the Revolutionary War by high taxation. Tories in England were controlled by clergy and wealthy landowners, who also tended to control local administration of justice. By occupation, the Republican-Democrat followers of Jefferson were more like Tories than Whigs and were, for the most part, farmers and southern plantation owners. Jefferson and the Republican-Democrats would have been highly insulted to hear themselves compared to the Tories, but there was another similarity which caused the Tories and the Republican-Democrats to be strong parties, while the Whigs and the Federalists were weak parties. The Tory Party was founded on the principle of divine right of kings, which made it the strong political party of England. The sovereignty of England is in its royalty.

The sovereignty of the United States is in the people of America, which the Republican-Democrats claimed to represent, while the Federalists were more interested in money and political and economic theory. In all of this, no consideration was made of people who did not join either party. It was just assumed that independent voters had lost their power in government, since the majority of voters had joined political parties.

In comparing American political parties with the English parties they were patterned after, it was the question of slavery that made American parties different from English parties. In England, the Whig Party led out in the abolitionist movement, soon joined by the Tory Party in abolishing slavery in the British empire in 1834. In America the Republican-Democrat Party became the Democratic Party started by Andrew Jackson and Martin van Buren, a pro-slavery party which started the Civil War. The Federalists disbanded and re-organized whenever they became particularly unpopular as National Republicans, Whigs, and finally as Republicans, choosing the right side of the slavery issue and winning the Civil War, but immediately afterward returning to their first great love, money.

The English Whig Party lost control of the English economy and became the English Liberal Party of today. Democrats in America call themselves liberals. The Tory Party became the Conservative Party and is now the party which controls England's money. Republicans in America call themselves conservatives.

In their imitation of English politics, Republicans of today can never really be like Conservatives of England because they do not have a monarch. Democrats are the party of popularity. When slavery was popular, they were a strong pro-slavery party. After the Civil War, they aligned themselves with the labor movement and other organizations of faction resulting from economic and political inequalities, making them today a party with an agenda copied from European socialists.

Chapter 5

The reasons that Jefferson and Hamilton gave for their political division may seem somewhat irrelevant today, both sides seeming to be antiquated by today's standard. Hamilton was using the power of government to enrich his Federalist friends by clever financial ideas. Almost all of Hamilton's schemes seemed to be at the expense of the farmers and plantation owners who supported Jefferson's party. The original difference still exists in government today.

In 1978 farmers in America were in hard times. Egged on by a farmer's union, farmers from all over America drove their tractors to Washington, D.C., to protest the economic conditions farmers were laboring under and to petition the government for relief. So Washington, D.C., was inundated with tractors clogging up traffic and angering people against farmers, which may have been one reason why government officials refused to listen in any way to these farm tractor protesters. David Stockman, President Reagan's economic advisor, summed up the attitude of

Washington, D.C., toward farmers.

If farmers could not follow good business practices, he said, they must face the consequences. So the farmers drove their tractors home minus the money they had spent on fuel to make the trip, and many of them lost their farms to the banks they had borrowed money from.

Contrast that reaction to farm foreclosures to the house foreclosure problem of 2008. Bank executives converged on Washington D.C. in their Lear jets, petitioned the government for relief, and left with 750 billion dollars, the first of several stimulus packages given directly to banks, some of which immediately used the money for bonuses given to bank executives.

Does it appear that political parties have solved the problem that they used to justify their existence in America?

The bank bailout was supported by both major parties of today. Times have changed. But in 1800 the basic similarity between the two parties was less defined. For one thing, in 1800 all voters were still independent voters. Voters just registered to vote, not as members of political parties. In their opposition to

Hamilton's financial policies, Jefferson and Madison hit on the idea of "caucuses", the extra-legal use of elected public officials for party organization. This idea was so successful that the Federalists were obliterated. It also created a problem in the electoral college that Congress was unable to resolve.

The Republican-Democrats decided to run two candidates for President because under the Constitution, each elector in the electoral college voted for two candidates for President, the candidate receiving the most votes being elected President and the candidate receiving the second most voters being elected Vice-President. This system, which had worked fine in electing Washington and Adams, and then Adams and Jefferson, was not adaptable to party politics. The Republican-Democrats ran Jefferson for President and Aaron Burr for Vice-President, so when Republican-Democrat electors cast their ballots in the electoral college, they all voted for two candidates, Jefferson and Burr, for President. If Republican-Democrats had put any thought into what they were doing, one of them would have voted for Jefferson and someone besides Burr, but it did not happen, so there was a tie vote in the electoral college. This threw the election into the House of Representatives to be decided, where Federalist votes went for Burr, and it took thirty-six ballots before Jefferson was finally elected.

Members of Congress considered this to be such a traumatic experience that they decided to make the office of Vice-President an office to be appointed by political parties, rather than an office elected by the people, starting the running-mate system still in effect today. It is typical of political parties that once the first successful party candidates for President and Vice-President were elected, no consideration has been made since that time except the running mate idea they started. A look at the actual amendment passed by Congress shows that a Vice-President cannot be elected by the people.

> XII. The electors shall meet in their respective States and vote by ballot for President and Vice-President, one of whom shall not be an inhabitant of the same State with themselves; they shall name in their ballots the person voted for as President and in distinct ballots the person voted for as Vice-President, and they shall make

distinct lists of all persons voted for as
President and of all persons voted for as
Vice-President, and of the number of votes
for each, which lists they shall sign and
certify, and transmit sealed to the seat of
the government of the United States,
directed to the President of the Senate.

The President of the Senate shall, in
the presence of the Senate and House of
Representatives, open all the certificates
and the votes shall then be counted. The
person having the greatest number of votes
for President shall be President, if such
number be a majority of the whole number
of electors appointed; and if no person
have such majority, then from the persons
having the highest numbers not exceeding
three on the list of those voted for as
President, the House of Representatives
shall choose immediately, by ballot, the
President. But in choosing the President
the votes shall be taken by States, the
representation from each State having one
vote; a quorum for this purpose shall

consist of a member or members from two thirds of the States, and a majority of all the States shall be necessary to a choice. And if the House of Representatives shall not choose a President whenever the right of choice shall devolve upon them, before the fourth day of March next following, then the Vice-President shall act as President, as in the case of the death or other constitutional disability of the President.

The person having the greatest number of votes as Vice-President shall be Vice-President, if such number be a majority of the whole number of electors appointed; and if no person have a majority, then from the two highest numbers on the list the Senate shall choose the Vice-President; a quorum for the purpose shall consist of two thirds of the whole number of Senators, and a majority of the whole number shall be necessary to a choice. But no person constitutionally ineligible to the office of President shall be eligible to that of Vice-President of the

United States.

Did I mention that members of Congress had been traumatized by the election of 1800?

What exactly does this amendment mean?

It means that an independent voter cannot be elected Vice-President of the United States as long as there are political parties. John Adams was an independent voter when he was elected Vice-President. Thomas Jefferson was still an independent voter when he was elected Vice-President. But Amendment XII insures that candidates for Vice-President cannot be elected unless they are running mates to Presidential candidates. In my opinion, independent voters should concede the office of Vice-President to political parties until such time as a better amendment can be made and only run candidates for President. Then the Presidential campaign of an independent candidate for President cannot be dragged down by the requirements of Amendment XII. An independent President can be elected. A political party Vice-President can be elected to the office that one political party Vice-President said was not worth a bucket of warm spit, and the nation can move forward. John

Adams seemed to think that the office of Vice-President was a good one when he was an independent Vice-President. Congress could have continued on with the kind of elections that had elected Washington and Adams. All they had to do was give the electoral college or the House of Representatives a better means of breaking a tie vote. They could have said, If there is a tie vote, there will be two more votes, one to select a President and one to select a Vice-President. There was no reason to make it as complicated as they did except that since they had been so traumatized by thirty-six votes in the House, they could not wait to turn the responsibility of selecting the Vice-President over to political parties. They accomplished in American government what had been accomplished in English government during the reign of Queen Anne, a law mandating the existence of political parties.

Notwithstanding their success at taking over the government with their political party, Jefferson and his Vice-President were not off to a good start with each other. As it became known to Burr that Jefferson was not going to have him as his running mate in 1804, he decided to run for governor of New York as an independent. Due to remarks that Alexander Hamilton had made concerning his candidacy for governor, Burr challenged Hamilton to a duel.

After their meeting on the political party field of honor, Hamilton was dead, and Burr was wanted in two states for murder, which did not do a lot for his Vice-Presidency. It was at this point that Burr became interested in an enterprise on the borders of Mexico, which would establish a new nation in which Burr might conceivably get a better job than Vice-President of the United States. Accordingly, Burr and some disaffected persons he had recruited started down the Ohio River on flatboats on their way to some nameless glory. The enterprise collapsed when President Jefferson had them arrested and tried for treason. The Republican-Democrat Party may have secured the office of Vice-President to themselves, but their first Vice-President could scarcely be called a success.

One reason we might want to remember the first political party Vice-President is his fleet of flatboats, probably the first party platform in America.

Chapter 6

If Thomas Jefferson had been told that he was starting a political party that one day would be instrumental in a trillion dollar bailout of banks at the expense of the taxpayers, he would have thought he was conversing with an insane person. All of the ideals he supported and proposed and that his party stood for were designed to prevent that kind of occurrence in government. The fact is, life under Jefferson's dominating party did not seem so much different from life under independent Presidents Washington and Adams. After all, Jefferson was the man who had written the Declaration of Independence. He ought to be able to keep the people of the United States independent. So the United States essentially had one party government through the administrations of Jefferson, Madison, and Monroe. The Federalists still existed, but in a severely weakened state, and offered up sacrificial lambs as candidates to be defeated by the Republican-Democrats until the Federalists officially gave up the ghost in 1816, and Monroe ran unopposed in 1820.

The next election in 1824 resulted in four Republican-Democrat candidates, John Quincy Adams, Andrew Jackson, William Crawford, and Henry Clay, who split the vote, throwing the election into the House of Representatives. John Quincy Adams and Henry Clay combined their support on the promise that Clay would become Secretary of State in the administration of Adams, earning them the election and the everlasting hatred of Andrew Jackson. Adams and Clay then started the National Republican Party, which after a time took the name of Whig Party.

Andrew Jackson won the popular vote in 1824, but lost the election in the House. In 1828 the hero of the Battle of New Orleans was ready for his opposition. The National Republican administration of John Quincy Adams had been based on public works projects, the most notable of which had been the Erie Canal, which made for a stable but unexciting four years. The election of 1828 was the first election with modern party campaigning. Jackson supporters appeared everywhere with brass bands, electioneering, and party promotion. John Quincy Adams lost the election by a substantial margin.

It was also the first election in which the news media took its place as the organ of party propaganda. The election of 1828 is remembered for its mudslinging in the press by both parties.

From the time of Jefferson until Jackson, the office of Vice-President was in a state of limbo. Presidential candidates appeared in different states with different Vice-Presidential candidates, sometimes as many as five or six nationwide for one Presidential candidate. In 1824 John C. Calhoun was the Vice-Presidential candidate for all four Presidential candidates in various parts of the country, and so ended up as John Quincy Adams' Vice-President. In the same election, Andrew Jackson won votes in the electoral college for both President and Vice-President. None of the elections for Vice-President were decided in the Senate the way the twelfth amendment describes until 1836. In 1828 Vice-President John C. Calhoun switched to the Democratic Party and was elected as Jackson's Vice-President after serving in the same office for John Quincy Adams.

Once Andrew Jackson was in office, he began to consolidate his followers into a modern political party, changing the name of the party from Republican-

Democrat Party to Democratic Party. His greatest help in this effort was his first Secretary of State and second Vice-President, Martin van Buren. Van Buren and Jackson were the first American politicians to mount a campaign to convince Americans that political parties were necessary in the United States government, Van Buren even writing a book on the subject. The strength of the Democrats lay in Jackson's personal popularity and in organization of faction at local level; brass bands, party campaigning, and promoting local, state, and national Democratic candidates together. The result was a pro-slavery party that dominated in western and southern states. It was an unfortunate time for such a party to be formed. English political parties had just abolished slavery in the British empire.

The other thing Jackson did during his Presidency was to mount a campaign against the National Bank. In this campaign Jackson was also successful, breaking the bank and changing United States monetary policy. Jackson is another party politician who would never believe that the party he started gave almost a trillion dollars of public revenues to banks that were threatening to shut down after the election of 2008.

Perhaps the most significant political party action during Jackson's Presidency was the action of a minor party, the Anti-Masonic Party, which held the first party convention and selected William Wirt as its candidate for President. The Democrats were quick to copy this method of selecting a candidate by holding a convention in 1835 to select Martin van Buren as their candidate for President and Richard M. Johnson as their candidate for Vice-President.

Martin van Buren, the little magician, was elected in 1836. His Vice-Presidential candidate, Johnson, fell one vote short of having a majority in the electoral college, and is the only Vice-President to be elected by the Senate according to the provisions of Amendment XII. The Whigs purposely ran four candidates against Van Buren, hoping to throw the Presidential election into the House. The strategy failed, and Van Buren was elected with a majority of votes in the electoral college. Unfortunately for Van Buren, there was a financial panic in 1837, which the Whigs blamed on Van Buren and Jackson and their campaign against the National Bank.

The Whigs held their first party convention in the election of 1840. Whig candidate William Henry

Harrison defeated Van Buren. Harrison only lived a short time after his election, and his Vice-President, John Tyler, became the first Vice-President to advance to the Presidency on the death of a President. The 1840's and 1850's were a period of political indecision for the American people, alternating back and forth between Jackson's strong pro-slavery party and Henry Clay's weak Whig Party, as the dominant political issue became the question of slavery in the United States.

Since political party politicians in America today do little except copy what they see political party politicians do in European governments, it is too bad that there was only one American party trying to emulate Whigs and Tories of England during the 1830's. The Democrats of that time were engaged with Mexico and paying more attention to French and Spanish politics with regard to slaves than acts of Parliament. Henry Clay's weak Whig Party was making a half-hearted opposition to slavery in the United States. Henry Clay's idea of opposition was compromise, the Missouri Compromise, the Kansas-Nebraska Compromise, the Compromise of 1850, etc., etc. In the meantime, Whigs and Tories in England had long since abolished slavery in the British empire. The anti-slavery movement was becoming stronger all the time in the United States, especially in New England, with no practical means of expression in government under Whig Party and Democratic Party corruption.

Briefly, the 1840's and 1850's went like this. Democrat James Polk was elected in 1844. Whig candidate Zachary Taylor was elected in 1848. Taylor soon died, and his Vice-President, Millard Fillmore, become President. Democrat Franklin Pierce was elected in 1852, and Democrat James Buchanan was elected in 1856. The Whig Party fizzled out between 1852 and 1856, not even selecting a candidate at its last convention but voting to support Millard Fillmore, who was the candidate of the American Party. One Whig splinter group started the Republican Party and ran as its candidate the western explorer John Fremont in an anemic first attempt.

By 1860 the anti-slavery elements of the United States had decided to consolidate their efforts by uniting in the Republican Party. This led to the nomination of Abraham Lincoln, who had become the best spokesman for the anti-slavery movement during his unsuccessful campaign against Democrat Stephen A. Douglas for the United States Senate.

For the first time in American politics, there was a distinct moral difference between the two prevailing parties. The Democrats were pro-slavery; the Republicans were anti-slavery. The Democrats held a substantial numerical advantage, but a less united front. Given the makeup of the two parties and the condition of the legislative branch of government, there was little possibility of resolving the issue of slavery in a peaceful manner.

England had not experienced this difficulty in resolving the slave question because England had a unifying factor, the churches of England. The churches of England taught that slavery was inhuman. The Whigs in Parliament initiated the idea of abolition of slavery. The Tories and Whigs discussed the issue in Parliament in a heated manner, weighing the moral objectives against the economic realities. In the end, the will of the people of England prevailed because Englishmen, including their king, did not like slavery and decided as a people that slavery was inhuman. The two-party system worked with regard to slavery in England because, as George Washington had pointed out, political parties could sometimes be beneficial in governments of a monarchical cast.

In the American system, political parties had the opposite effect. The churches here did not have a unifying effect. While churches in the northern states were teaching that slavery was inhuman the same as churches in England, churches in the southern states were teaching that slavery was the means by which the souls of black people could be saved. Then, too, the Apostle Paul had told escaped slave Onesimus in the Bible to return to his master. Working class Americans identified more with the working slaves than with their idle masters, but most of them were also members of the pro-slavery Democratic Party, started by their hero, Andrew Jackson. By nature, most Americans were opposed to slavery, but how can the direction of a pro-slavery party be changed?

The conduct of political parties in pre-Civil War America was in part attributable to the desire of Americans to be subject to military leadership. The first strong party leader, Andrew Jackson, was a duel fighting, horse racing, hard campaigning, tactical genius military leader who carried his military style into his Presidency and into his campaign against the national bank. If Andy Jackson had slaves, then maybe slavery was not so bad, because one thing was certain, Jackson was a military leader worthy to be Commander in Chief of the United States military. The Whigs were quick to pick up on this attitude and began to nominate war heroes almost exclusively, William Henry Harrison, Zachary Taylor, and Winfield Scott. The militarism of the time was further heightened by the Mexican War, which the Whig Party opposed. Democratic President James Polk started the War, but Whig Generals Taylor and Scott won it.

So the two-party system in the United States had become a pro-slavery military discipline going in one direction and a defensive anti-slavery movement going in the opposite direction which would inevitably collide. When the Democrats split their vote in the 1860 Presidential election between Democratic candidate Stephen A. Douglas and a southern Democrat, John Breckenridge, Republican Abraham Lincoln was elected.

In their military manner, seven southern states seceded from the United States during the time between the election of 1860 and the inauguration of Lincoln and declared themselves to be the Confederate states of America. Outgoing Democratic President James Buchanan dithered in the White House wishing that inauguration day would arrive. Upon entering the office of President, Lincoln did not recognize the Confederacy or any right to secede, but seemed to be willing to leave it at that, making no move to force the issue. This made the militaristic Confederates a little impatient, so they attacked Fort Sumter at Charleston, South Carolina, and the Civil War was on.

Would there have been a Civil War if Americans had heeded the advice of President George Washington and not divided into political parties?

The answer is, No.

Without political parties the issue of slavery would have been resolved. Americans, except for wealthy southern plantation owners, had no use for slaves or slavery. The working poor and small farmers in the South who did not own slaves, were pulled into the war on the side of slavery because they were told the war was about states rights. To some extent it was true. States had more rights before the war than they had after it. States lost rights because southern states seceded from the Union, not because northern states were trying to take rights away. If southerners had really been concerned about states rights, they would have recognized the right of individual states to make their own decisions about slavery instead of trying to impose laws relating to slavery on all states. The poorer classes in the South lost their right to be civilians when the Confederate government, which came from the Democratic Party started by Andrew Jackson, attacked Fort Sumter.

Whereas, political parties gave England a means of abolishing slavery, political parties in America kept Americans from abolishing slavery without a war. Same result, but one way was better than the other. Just taking a vote is a lot less messy.

Chapter 7

Abraham Lincoln had hoped up until the time Fort Sumter was attacked that war could be avoided. It could have been, but his political party would not allow it. If he had told the seven seceding states, "Well, you have left the United States. Goodbye, and good luck.", then there would have been no war. However, party politicians had gone through a little taste of secession during the Presidency of Andrew Jackson. South Carolina had voted to nullify a federal law and had threatened to secede from the United States. Consequently, party politicians in the North were already agreed that under no circumstances would a state be allowed to leave the nation once it was a state of the United States.

Militarily, Fort Sumter was of no value to the Union or the Confederacy. In terms of law, if the South attacked the fort, it would be no different from Cuba attacking Guantanamo today. The present government of Cuba did not give the United States permission to have a military base at Guantanamo, but they have never attacked it. The truth was that the South thought they could win a war with the North, much the same as Japan thought they could defeat the United States before World War II. There was a reason for this sentiment. Most of the graduates of West Point were from the South. The best high ranking officers in the United States military had gone with the Confederacy. The north was left with a skeleton army, while the South filled the ranks of their army with the call, "Come on, boys, we are going to defend states rights. Follow General Lee."

In the end, Lincoln was the only one defending states rights. The Constitution is very clear about war. Congress shall have power to declare war. The President shall be Commander in Chief of the armed forces. The President issued a declaration after Fort Sumter was attacked declaring that the southern states were in a state of insurrection which would require the United States military to suppress. The declaration called Congress back into session to raise and equip an army of 85,000 to deal with the problem. It was not a declaration of war. Congress has sole power to declare war. Lincoln dealt with the problem this way so that the states in rebellion officially remained part of the

United States. Once the war was won, it would be easier to restore them to their previous status in the government. Lincoln's miscalculation was in how difficult it would be to suppress the rebellion. For its part, Congress met and began to raise an army in which the wealthy could pay people less fortunate to take their places in the ranks. Military contracts were awarded to friends and associates of Congressmen, and wormy flour and broken down horses were provided to the new troops.

It took only a few battles with the well-led Confederate army before the Union army was starting to learn the realities of war.

In studying the role of American political parties in putting together this conflict, we have so far only considered the Executive branch of government and its role in the division of the country. It is interesting to note that in 1860 the two party system had elected the best President they had elected up to that time. Lincoln was not like previous Presidents, trying to appease both sides of the slavery question. He took a definite stand against slavery and called it a moral wrong, so states started seceding from the Union. In Congress, where issues like slavery are supposed to be resolved, nothing was done about slavery from the start of the United States until the Civil War. The Constitution mentions slavery, not because the framers of the Constitution were approving slavery, but because there were states where slavery existed, and the Constitutional convention had no way of resolving the matter. It would have to be resolved in the United States Congress and state governments after the United States was a nation. The reason why it was not resolved was because the nation divided into political parties, and Congress was so weakened by that division that it could no longer deal with any important matters like slavery. When King Charles II started two-party corruption in England, he did it for the purpose of weakening Parliament. Two-party corruption accomplished its purpose in England. Parliament is getting weaker all the time. But the weakness of Parliament is nothing compared to the weakness Congress became after 1800. First, Congress could not resolve the problem that a political party presented in wanting to control both top offices of the United States. There was no reason to make it as complicated as they did , except that they had decided to have a two-party system of political corruption, and obtaining the office of Vice-President for political parties was essential to their plan.

The Constitution was intended from the beginning to be amended from time to time as the need arose. Political parties quickly made it almost impossible to amend the Constitution or even pass necessary legislation by incorporating a multitude of party positions into Congressional procedure. As George Washington predicted, the administration of Congress has been the mirror of ill-conceived projects of faction according to the alternate triumphs of different parties.

It would be incorrect to say that all party politicians elected to Congress have been corrupt. However, enough of them have been that it has been a dire situation since the time political parties took over the government. The only time the people get a look into the seriousness of the situation is when corrupt politicians of one party anger the corrupt politicians of the other enough to trigger a corruption sting.

As pertaining to slavery, Congress could do nothing but compromise with regard to new states and territories admitted to the union, whether they would be admitted as free or slave states. That was all that was done in Congress concerning slavery until the Civil War. After the Civil War started, Congress could have proposed emancipation of slaves, but they did not. They were too busy trying to make money for themselves and their friends in financing of the war. It took a Proclamation from the President to free the slaves. With regard to the important issue of slavery, Congress became a judicial body, not a legislative one, judging whether new states would be free or slave. They judged that slavery was going to continue until forced to do otherwise when the Confederates lost the Civil War. Then they had no choice but to prohibit slavery in all states.

That brings us to the third branch of government, the judicial branch. The Constitution sets the jurisdiction and limits of the Supreme Court. Political parties changed it. With a ruling that the Supreme Court had a duty to rule on all legislation from Congress to determine its Constitutionality, the Supreme Court had embarked on its legislative agenda. Slavery gave the court its greatest opportunity to legislate from the bench. The Dred Scott decision was the last Supreme Court decision regarding slavery and shows what the Supreme Court was doing with regard to writing laws.

Dred Scott was in a free state, but had to be returned to his owner in a slave state, said the Supreme Court. With regard to any other kind of fugitive, the practice of extradition had to be followed. The state seeking custody had to convince a court in the state where the person was to hand over the person. The Supreme Court was attempting to say that a slave was a slave anywhere in the United States because slavery was mentioned in the Constitution and was therefore the law of the land.

But the Supreme Court was completely out of their jurisdiction because slaves were people who had been kidnapped from their homes in Africa or who were descendants of people who had been kidnapped. There was no contract or agreement between slaves and the people they were working for. To apply the reasoning of the Taney Supreme Court to two modern day kidnappings, when Elizabeth Smart tried to escape from her kidnappers, they had a right to secure her to a cable because they had told her that she was their slave. Or in the other recent case, the two daughters of Jaycee Dugard had to stay in the back yard with their mother because she was a slave, and that made them slaves.

The arguments being used in court before the Civil War to uphold slavery were no less ridiculous. While slavery is no longer the Constitution of the United States in the judgment of the Supreme Court because Congress was forced to write the Thirteenth Amendment, the courts today still control the people by saying that they have the right to impose other inhuman practices. Originally, the Supreme Court was intended to hear and decide individual specific cases, the decision of each case applying to that particular case. By making the Supreme Court the legislative body of the land, each case that goes before the court is now thought to be a law unto itself. The decisions of lower courts are also individual laws, depending on their agreement with Supreme Court decisions. This is all what lawyers and judges of today call "case law". They have plenty of case law. What they are lacking is what the Taney Supreme Court lacked, common sense. Because the Supreme Court made case law stronger than acts of Congress, the judicial branch of government is now the strongest branch of government instead of the weakest as was intended. The legislative branch is the weakest, doing almost nothing that needs to be done.

Chapter 8

Once the Confederate states had the war they wanted so badly, it was only a matter of time before they lost it, as it turned out, a long time. Lincoln elevated a young general named George McClellan to command the Army of the Potomac in the East. McClellan was a brilliant organizer, probably the best person in the nation to overcome the problems of supply originating with a corrupt Congress, one of the reasons he was so popular with his troops. But there were some problems with McClellan. First of all, he was a pro-slavery Democrat, a supporter of Stephen A. Douglas in the election of 1860, differing with Southern Democrats only on the issue of the right of states to secede. Second, he was insubordinate, especially toward General-in-Chief Winfield Scott, who had planned the conduct of the war with what proved to be the winning strategy, a naval blockade of the South and a river based campaign on the Mississippi River designed to split the Confederate states in half. McClellan wanted a campaign with the Confederate capitol, Richmond, as its objective. Conditions became so acrimonious between the two Generals that the aged General Scott eventually submitted his resignation to Lincoln, and McClellan was elevated to the position of General-in-Chief, still retaining his command of the Army of the Potomac. This suited McClellan just fine, and he continued to build and train a huge army in the East, but did little with it. He transferred his insubordinate attitude toward the President, making Lincoln wait before receiving him any time the President went to see him.

McClellan had only one major engagement with the Confederate army, the battle of Antietam, while Generals Grant and Sherman were making good progress in the west with Winfield Scott's plan to divide the Confederacy by controlling the Mississippi River. Lincoln replaced McClellan as General-in-Chief with a succession of Union Generals, none of whom could win a battle against Robert E. Lee until Lee made a mistake in tactics against Union General George Meade at the battle of Gettysburg, Pennsylvania, and suffered a major defeat. At this point, Lincoln could see the light at the end of the tunnel and placed Grant over the army in the east while Sherman went into Georgia from the west, and it was only a matter of time before the South had taken enough punishment and decided to surrender.

In the meantime, the election of 1864 took place in which the Democrats ran pro-slavery military candidate George McClellan against Republican incumbent Abraham Lincoln. Fortunately for America, Lincoln was re-elected.

On April 15, 1865, President Lincoln was assassinated by a pro-slavery stage actor, John Wilkes Booth.

In the final analysis we can see that the pro-slavery advocates all had something in common with the black slaves who labored under slavery's cruel domination. General Robert E. Lee, as he led his troops into battle, the southern plantation owners who had the slaves, the poor southern boys who served in the Confederate army, Chief Justice Roger Taney as he wrote the opinion for the Dred Scott case, John Wilkes Booth as he pulled the trigger of the gun that killed the President, all of them could tell that slavery was an inhuman practice. There was no one in America who could not tell that slavery was wrong. So why did

Americans in the southern states and many in the north, including the Democratic candidate for President and the man who assassinated President Lincoln, say they were in favor of slavery?

It was a manifestation of what President George Washington called "the baneful effects of the spirit of party". They were letting a political party do their thinking for them. Having set their hearts and lives on a party agenda, they were incapable of taking another course, even to the extreme taken by John Wilkes Booth and his fellow conspirators after the Confederacy had lost the war.

The effects of the spirit of party were no less evident among the anti-slavery victors of the war. While President Lincoln set forth the best kind of example to the people in his Second Inaugural Address, advocating "malice toward none and charity for all", the Radical Republicans in Congress were in favor of punishment, retribution, and revenge. With the assassination of the President, the Radical Republicans opposed the new President, Andrew Johnson, in every effort he made to follow Lincoln's ideas for reconstruction, finally impeaching Johnson and failing to remove him from office by only one vote.

The result was a reconstruction policy that was based on party corruption, with carpetbaggers from the north descending on Southern states in search of the spoils of war, and scalawags, or southern counterparts in corruption, cheating their own neighbors to share in the dishonesty of the carpetbaggers.

In 1868 Republican candidate Ulysses S. Grant was elected President of the United States and also re-elected in 1872. The Grant administration contained more party corruption than any administration up to that time. It also precipitated a financial panic in 1873, which lasted until 1879. Grant's talent for military leadership did not extend over into his efforts in farming, business, and politics, where he had a tendency to be a failure.

The controversial election of 1876 saw Republican Rutherford B. Hayes elected President over Democrat Samuel B. Tilden by one electoral vote after Tilden won the popular vote. The electoral votes of four states numbering twenty-two votes were in dispute, and a Congressional Commission decided all twenty-two votes would go to Hayes. Democrats started calling Hayes by the name of Rutherfraud. For his part, Hayes stated the political sentiment of the time in his campaign slogan, He serves his party best who serves his country best.

This is a little different from George Washington's statement that it is the duty of all Americans to discourage political parties.

In 1880 Republican James Garfield was elected over Democrat Winfield Scott Hancock, two Civil War generals running against one another. Garfield was assassinated by a disappointed office seeker shortly after taking office, and his Vice-President, Chester A. Arthur, became President.

In 1884 Andrew Jackson's "necessary" political party came back into power for the first time since before the Civil War. Democratic candidate Grover Cleveland was elected over Republican James G. Blaine. In 1888 Cleveland won the popular vote, but lost the electoral vote to Benjamin Harrison, the Republican candidate. Cleveland was re-elected in 1892 over Harrison, with 22 electoral votes going to a Populist Party candidate.

In 1896 Republican candidate William McKinley spent five times as much money as his opponent, William Jennings Bryan, who was running as the candidate of two parties, the Democratic Party and the Populist Party. Bryan, for his part, embarked on a speaking tour across the United States. This election was the beginning of modern day politics in which the parties began to raise large amounts of money to promote their candidates in the news media, and the candidates began to openly pay for media exposure. McKinley was elected.

On April 25th, 1898, Congress declared war against Spain after the battleship Maine exploded and sank in Havana harbor in Cuba. As a result of this war, the United States obtained the Philippines, Puerto Rico, and Guam. This led to an American-Philippine conflict, during which some of the worst atrocities ever perpetrated by American soldiers took place.

McKinley was re-elected in 1900 after another campaign against Bryan, but assassinated in 1901 by an anarchist, and Theodore Roosevelt, the Vice-President, became President.

As far as the legislative and judicial branches were concerned, suffice it to say that the period of time between the Civil War and the turn of the century was the time when corruption in these two branches of government became a way of life.

Chapter 9

It is not as though American political parties were breaking new ground in government. What they actually did was to make American government the mirror of bad European policy. I have described how the two-party system of political corruption that controls the United States originated in English government. As George Washington described, in monarchical governments political parties can sometimes be the means by which the people can be heard, and so, according to Washington, they can somewhat be justified in European governments, which were almost all monarchies when Washington made his comments. During the 1800's European political parties took two different forms, given the designation of left-wing and right-wing in European politics. Right–wing parties aligned themselves with the nationalism of nations, during this time usually in support of monarchy, while left-wing parties opposed monarchy, often in favor of socialistic or communistic ideals. Germany and Italy were nations that developed strong nationalistic parties during the 1800's, while most European nations had left-wing parties opposed to monarchy.

In 1848 Karl Marx and Friedrich Engels were commissioned by the Communist League of Europe to write a book setting forth Communist ideals. Their book, the Communist Manifesto, called for an overthrow, not only of European monarchy, but also of all wealthy people, called the bourgeois by the Communists. This was to be accomplished by an armed revolution of working class and poor people, who were called the proletariat.

From the left-wing parties of Europe came the labor union movement, a less extreme attempt to improve the lives of the working class in industrial society than Communism, but sometimes also connected to Communism. The labor union movement was also mirrored in American politics during the industrial revolution. The Democratic Party became the party in America aligned with labor unions, while the Republican Party aligned itself with money and wealth once their original goal of abolition of slavery was accomplished by the Civil War. The party alignment with these classes of society actually goes back to the time of Thomas Jefferson and the Republican-Democrats and Alexander Hamilton and the Federalists and has to do with the method each party used to gain support of the voters. The Republicans, like the Federalists from whom they had evolved, liked to organize their party by financial means, using the government as a means of obtaining a financial advantage. The Democrats, like the Republican-Democrats from whom they came, liked direct organization of faction of the kind George Washington predicted, creation of dissenting factions which are then incorporated into party structure. One segment of society excepted from this was slaves, but once slavery was abolished, the Democrats portrayed themselves as the party of the common people, while they portrayed the Republicans as the party of the rich, so most black people today are members of the party that started as a pro-slavery party. The Democratic Party of today likes to present itself as the only voice in government for the disadvantaged.

Political parties in Europe were the antithesis of independence. Whether nationalistic or socialistic in nature, European parties made the people dependent on the state.

One thing that made America different was the west, wide open spaces where there were but few people. In order to encourage settlement of the west, Abraham Lincoln had encouraged passage of the Homestead Act of 1862. A person in the United States could claim enough land to make a good sized farm and obtain title to the land by building a livable house and making other improvements within a certain time. Members of Congress from the South had opposed homesteading because it would insure that western states admitted to the Union would be free instead of slave states. With the beginning of the Civil War and secession of the southern states, Lincoln was able to get the Homestead Act passed, giving Americans an economic and social independence that did not exist in any other country. Americans who felt oppressed in the eastern United States under political party control could get a team and wagon and go west where things were more independent.

The bad thing about this kind of independence was that it made Americans somewhat apolitical, leaving a huge group of Americans who did not even vote. The word independent came to be associated with people who did not participate in elections. The

Constitution of the United States left it to the states to determine the requirements for political candidacy. While such requirements at first were to just register with the state or local government, as political parties began to gain more control over elections, other requirements were added, such as nomination petition signatures, filing fees, etc., all designed to exclude independent voters from being candidates for office. After a while it was just accepted that independent voters could not be elected to office except in unusual circumstances, such as when political parties had made the people especially angry. Starting with the office of Vice-President, political parties made requirements for candidacy to high offices too difficult for anyone but a party candidate with party backing to be elected. States like North Carolina, which had a high number of independent voters from the beginning, also had high nomination petition requirements for independent voters which prevented any independent voters except those who were wealthy enough to meet the requirements to get on the ballot. States with fewer independent voters tended to keep the candidacy requirements lower, since no independent voter was going to be elected anyway.

With the beginning of political party conventions in the 1830's, the division between political parties became more pronounced. It was still up to each individual state to decide the manner and form for registration of its voters. There is still one state, North Dakota, in which voters are not required to register. This points to the difficulty that American political parties had in the beginning in consolidating their power. The ideal situation for political parties is for the state government to require that the voter specify a party preference. At exactly what point and in which states this began to happen is unclear. My impression is that during the 1800's, voters just registered to vote. The modern differentiation into political party designations on the voter registration form seems to have started with primary elections, which were not invented until after the turn of the century. The spirit of party which divided Americans in the 1800's seemed to have a speculative rather than an administrative origin. When Americans went to the polls, they wanted to vote for the winning candidate. You would not go to a horse race and bet on the slowest horse. There were some who would vote for an independent or minor party candidate, but not many. The trick to party voting was to belong to a party which would win elections, or if it lost could at least say it made a good showing. That meant one of two major parties.

But it was not necessarily a given. The Federalist Party folded up. The Whig Party folded up. The Democrats backed the wrong horse in the Civil War and lost their popularity. The Republicans were caught cheating, and the Democrats became popular again. The problem was that in the minds of the people, political parties were the government of the United States. What determined which one would be in power was which one made the least serious mistakes.

The Populist movement at the end of the century brought about a change in party politics that was not for the better. Republican Party leadership did not want anything even resembling Populism to get started in their party. Republican candidates were to be chosen and controlled by Republican Party leaders. Democrats were more open to the idea of candidates coming from the people, but after unsuccessfully running Populist candidate William Jennings Bryan multiple times, they were open to suggestions. Conditions were in place for a major party power consolidation.

The answer was a set of elections to be paid for from public revenues in which the parties would consolidate power behind specific candidates before the general election. This cut independent voters out of the government entirely. To show how fair they were, political parties made some primary elections closed primaries in which only party members could vote and some primary elections open primaries in which independent voters could vote for party candidates, all to be paid for by the taxpayers. This was an Europeanization of American political parties which made the twentieth century a century in which independence was declining from start to finish.

Theodore Roosevelt was re-elected in 1904, his Democratic opponent Alton Parker only taking the southern states. Republican William Howard Taft defeated Democrat William Jennings Bryan, who was making his third attempt in 1908, and the Democrats joined the Republicans in putting together the system of primary elections that keeps all but politically elite party members from becoming candidates today. Democrat Woodrow Wilson was elected in 1912 when Teddy Roosevelt started the Bullmoose Party and split the Republican vote between Taft and him.

On 28 June 1914 the Archduke of Austria was assassinated by a Serbian extremist, starting World War I.

Chapter 10

As anyone who has studied European history might expect, the assassination of the Archduke of Austria by a Serbian ended up as a war between Germany and the United States. First Austria, Hungary, and Germany were fighting Serbia and Russia. Then Germany was fighting England and France. Then a German U-boat sank an American passenger ship, and the Americans had to send troops to Europe to win the war. Then the Germans surrendered without Germany being invaded, causing German Corporal Adolf Hitler to believe that somewhere in the High Command, Germany had been betrayed.

The Russians had a particularly bad time of it in World War I. They lost about a million soldiers fighting the Germans for Czar Nicholas II. Then there was a Communist revolution, the Bolsheviks killed the Czar and his family, and Russia became the Union of Soviet Socialist Republics.

With the War to End All Wars completed,

President Wilson started the League of Nations, but could not get Congress to authorize the United States to join.

In the election of 1920, Republican Warren G. Harding defeated Democratic candidate James G. Cox in a landslide. The Harding administration has the distinction of having the second most high ranking government officials of any administration end up in prison. To say that the Harding administration was corrupt is an understatement. Harding died from a heart attack in 1923 and was succeeded by Vice-President Calvin Coolidge. Coolidge was re-elected in 1924. Republican Herbert Hoover won a landslide victory against Democrat Al Smith in 1928.

During the 1920's the machinations of American political parties, while they may have seemed important to many Americans, were of little consequence in shaping the events to come. American political parties had tied themselves to European politics, and it was three European parties that would control the fate of the world for most of the remainder of the century. The first of these was the Communist Party, the party which arose from the writings of Karl Marx and which openly advocated revolution, overthrow of capitalism, and an eventual workers' paradise which could only be achieved under world Communism. The Soviet Union had resulted from an overthrow of the Czarist government of Russia, the first of what Communists hoped would be many Communist revolutions. Communism was the extreme left wing of European politics.

The other two significant parties were two nationalistic parties, the Fascists in Italy, which came into power in 1922 and whose leader, Benito Mussolini, shared power with the Italian king, Victor Emmanuel III. This was a party which was promoted in some mystical way as a recurrence of the glory of the Roman Empire. By itself it would probably never have amounted to much, but it helped bring into power and joined with another nationalistic party in Europe which did become a significant force. The other nationalistic party was the National Socialist Party of Germany, later known as the Nazi Party.

The National Socialists were a small socialist party which had the misfortune to be joined by a young former German soldier named Adolf Hitler. Hitler soon learned that he had a talent for making political speeches, and starting with his belief that Germany had been betrayed at the end of World War I, he was soon the dominant personality of the party. It was at this time that Hitler noticed the Fascist Party, which had just come into power in Italy, and patterned his party organization and path to power after what the Fascists had done. It did not work for Hitler's party, and Hitler ended up in jail.

Hitler's year in prison gave him time to organize his thoughts and write a book. After his release from incarceration, the organization of faction within his party was based on three primary things, German nationalism, anti-Semitism, and anti-Communism. The collapse of the German economy during the world wide economic depression after 1928 brought Hitler's Nazi Party into power. The Depression resulted in two huge political parties in Germany, the Communist Party and the Nazi Party. Since the Communist Party required a revolution to take control of the government, the Germans chose to elevate the Nazis, and German Communist Party members ended up being soldiers in the army of the Third Reich.

Chapter 11

When the stock market crashed in 1929, Herbert Hoover should have been the best qualified person in America to deal with the problem. During World War I, Hoover was leader of war relief in Europe, distributing food, clothing, and other necessities to victims of the war. After the war he was Secretary of Commerce in the administrations of Presidents Harding and Coolidge, dealing with disasters such as the great Mississippi River flood in 1927. But as unemployment skyrocketed, the President seemed almost paralyzed, the government immobilized by a deadlock between a Republican President and his Democratic Congress. In 1932 the people elected Democratic candidate Franklin D. Roosevelt in a landslide.

Roosevelt was re-elected in 1936. Progress in America against the Great Depression was slow. By 1939 unemployment was at about 10%, down from 24% in 1933, but still not good. However, the predominating political party in the 1930's was the Nazi Party of Germany. Runaway inflation brought an end to the German Weimar Republic and brought the Nazi Party into power. Hitler was appointed Chancellor of Germany in 1933. From this appointive office, Hitler maneuvered himself to the position of absolute dictator of Germany. Once in control of Germany, the Nazi Party employed the people in public works projects, persecution of Jews, and rearmament of Germany. The Axis Alliance of Germany and Italy eventually took over almost all of Europe by force.

Compare what happened in Germany to President George Washington's analysis of the effect political parties could have on elective governments, made in 1796.

"The disorders and miseries which result gradually incline the minds of men to seek security and repose in the absolute power of an individual, and sooner or later the chief of some prevailing faction, more able or more fortunate than his competitors, turns this disposition to the purposes of his own elevation, on the ruins of public liberty."

This was not the first time democracy had

become absolute dictatorship in Europe. The French Revolution had resulted in Napoleon Bonaparte and his attempt to conquer the world. The Nazi dictatorship was a particularly horrific dictatorship because of the attempt of the Nazis to exterminate all Jews in Europe.

In 1939 Japan was added to the Axis Powers by treaty. Two years later Japan drew the United States into World War II with an attack on United States naval forces at Pearl Harbor, Hawaii.

In 1936 Democratic incumbent Franklin Roosevelt defeated Republican Alf Landon in a landslide, and again in 1940 Roosevelt defeated Republican Wendell Wilkie. In 1944 Roosevelt defeated Republican Thomas E. Dewey. After the 1944 election, the 22nd Amendment was added to the Constitution limiting a United States President to two terms in office. Roosevelt died from a cerebral hemorrhage on April 15, 1945, and Harry S. Truman became President.

Fifteen days later Adolf Hitler committed suicide in his bunker in Berlin, as Soviet troops neared his position. British and United States troops were advancing from the other direction through western

Germany. President Truman ended the war with Japan by destroying two Japanese cities with atomic bombs in August of the same year. World War II resulted in about 60 million deaths, one third of which were military deaths and two thirds civilian deaths. Included in the 40 million civilian deaths were six million Jews killed in Nazi concentration camps.

Chapter 12

As we have seen, the two most prominent nationalistic parties in Europe did not provide their members with good leadership, even though they did all of the things that political parties do. They organized faction, they enfeebled the public administration, they initiated incongruous projects of faction, they elevated persons instead of principles of government, and they destroyed the liberty of the people. We shall now consider the other great party of Europe, the Communist Party, which had its origins in the industrialized nations of western Europe, but first overthrew the government of the eastern and less industrialized nation of Russia. The next Communist revolution began in the non-industrialized nation of China, but was put on hold while both sides fought the Japanese in World War II. After the war, the Communists finished taking over China. Russia had overrun many Eastern European countries in defeating the German army, and those overrun countries automatically became Communist satellite nations.

Finally, Communist North Korea moved its army into South Korea and drove the South Korean army and Americans in South Korea to the very southern tip of the Korean peninsula. President Truman ordered General Douglas McArthur to move American troops from occupied Japan into Korea, and the Korean Conflict was on. The Korean Conflict began in 1950. Harry Truman was still President because he had defeated Thomas Dewey in the election of 1948. The Korean Conflict ended in a stalemate at the 38th parallel after Communist China entered the war on the side of North Korea. The Korean Conflict was the first of many undeclared wars engaged in by the United States after World War II, the last time Congress declared war.

The Soviet Union had tested its first nuclear weapon in 1949, having learned how to make the device from Communist spies who worked on the American project to make the first atomic bomb. The United States and Russia engaged in a nuclear arms race throughout the 1950's and 60's, producing enough nuclear weapons to destroy all life on earth several times.

Republican candidate Dwight D. Eisenhower defeated Democrat Adlai Stevenson in 1952 and again in 1956. In 1959 Fidel Castro led a Communist overthrow of the government of Cuba.

Democrat John F. Kennedy defeated Republican Richard M. Nixon in 1960 for the Presidency. Kennedy encouraged a CIA led invasion of Cuba by Cuban refugees which was unsuccessful. The next year pictures taken by a United States spy plane showed that Russian ICBM missiles were being brought into Cuba. President Kennedy ordered a blockade of Cuba until the missiles were removed. President Kennedy was assassinated in November of 1963 in Dallas, Texas, by Lee Harvey Oswald, and Lyndon B. Johnson, the Vice President, became President. Johnson was re-elected in 1964 against Republican candidate Barry Goldwater.

When Johnson became President, there were 10,000 American military advisors in South Vietnam helping the South Vietnamese military against a Communist insurgency. Johnson increased the number of Americans in Vietnam to a total of 550,000 without a declaration of war. Eventually Americans were suffering more than 1,000 casualties per month.

The Civil Rights movement during Johnson's Presidency resulted in the Civil Rights Act of 1964 and the Voting Rights Act of 1965.

Republican Richard M. Nixon defeated Johnson's Vice-President, Hubert Humphrey, in the election of 1968. Nixon immediately opened peace talks with the North Vietnamese to end the Vietnam War. A cease fire was declared, and United States forces were withdrawn in 1973. But the re-election of Nixon against George McGovern in 1972 resulted in the Watergate scandal and Nixon's resignation in 1974 as he was replaced by Speaker of the House Gerald Ford. North Vietnam then broke the cease fire and overran the South Vietnamese army, taking South Vietnam in 1975.

Democrat Jimmy Carter defeated Republican Gerald Ford in 1976. The Carter Administration is remembered for poor economic times and for Americans held hostage at the American embassy in Iran. Carter was defeated by Republican Ronald Reagan in 1980.

The hostages were released, the economy improved, and a deranged man attempted to assassinate the President. Reagan was re-elected by a landslide in the election of 1984 against Democrat Walter Mondale. Reagan's second term started well with one on one talks with Soviet leader Mikhail Gorbachev, resulting in an agreement to reduce nuclear arms and, eventually, to the fall of the Berlin wall and the end of the Cold War. The latter part of Reagan's second term became embroiled in the Iran-Contra affair. Reagan learned that he was suffering from Alzheimer's disease before his second term ended.

Reagan's Vice-President, George H. W. Bush, was elected in 1988 over Democrat Michael Dukakis. In 1990 and 1991 the Mother of all Battles was fought in Kuwait after Iraq invaded that country, and American troops in Operation Desert Storm drove the Iraqis back into Iraq. George H. W. Bush was defeated in the election of 1992 by Democrat Bill Clinton.

During the early 1990's, Yugoslavia, the pride of European socialists and the nation which had consistently been held up to the world as the way socialism could benefit a nation erupted into civil war. First the Serbs were fighting the Croats. Then, as so often happens in Europe with people who look good, the Serbs started mass homicides of Bosnian Muslims in Bosnia and Albanians in Kosovo. President Clinton sent the American military to bomb the Serbs and stop the genocide.

Clinton was re-elected in 1996, defeating Republican Bob Dole. Clinton was impeached during his second term for obstruction of justice, but not convicted by the Senate.

Republican George W. Bush, son of President George H. W. Bush, was elected in 2000 against Democrat Al Gore in an election that was decided by the United States Supreme Court in a case involving disputed votes in the state of Florida. In 2001 the twin towers of the World Trade Center in New York City were destroyed by a terrorist attack, killing 2750 people. The President then sent United States troops to fight Al Qaeda and Taliban Muslim extremists in Afghanistan after it was determined that the suicide terrorists who had brought down the twin towers were from the Al Qaeda organization. American troops were later sent into Iraq. George W. Bush defeated Democrat John Kerry in the election of 2004.

Democrat Barack Obama was elected in 2008 against Republican John McCain after an economic crisis in the last year of George W. Bush's Presidency.

Chapter 13

In 2009, for the first time since 1800, there were more Americans claiming to be independent voters than Democrats, the largest political party in America since that election. This is a landmark in American politics that is significant, even though both major parties are pretending it did not happen and are going on with their party contentions as though it is just going to be business as usual from now on. To show how it is significant, we need to examine voter registration in one state, Arizona, because Arizona shows why independent voter registration will continue to be much greater than party registration.

In 1988 all deputy registrars in Arizona who were registered independent were dismissed and informed that they were no longer eligible to serve in that position. Deputy registrars were persons who were trained by County Recorders to register voters and authorized by the state to perform that function. Political party leadership had become concerned because in the election of 1986, for the first time in state history, independent voters had started to become deputy registrars in Arizona. The immediate cause of the dismissal was a House bill in the Arizona legislature, which was passed and signed into law by Governor Rose Mofford, requiring that deputy registrars in the state of Arizona be recommended by the chairman of a political party. After December 31, 1988, there were no longer any deputy registrars in the state who were registered independent.

It may seem strange to citizens of other states that political parties in Arizona would pay this much attention to independent deputy registrars. As the forty-eighth state admitted to the union, Arizona was a little deeper into two-party control than some states. In 1988 Arizona had about 200,000 independent voters who were prevented from voting in party primaries by closed primary elections. The majority of people in Arizona took great pride in not even being registered to vote, voter registration in 1988 standing at 48% of those eligible. Voter registration was watched closely in the state. Democrats in the state were the minority party and registered voters according to Democratic party organization of faction, the same as Democrats have always done everywhere. Since Republicans were the majority party, they registered voters according to the traditional Republican way, a method apparently taken from the Pharisees. They compassed sea and land to make one proselyte, preferably someone with money who could contribute financially to the party. Other than that, voter registration took care of itself. Independent deputy registrars did not appear to the leadership of either party to fit into this system of voter registration, especially with more than half the state not registered to vote. It was something for the state legislature to correct.

Usually this kind of political action went completely unnoticed. This time it did not. An independent voter in Glendale, Arizona, filed a lawsuit seeking re-instatement of independent deputy registrars. When the date for that court case approached a few years later, the two major parties took a surprising action. Evidently not wanting to discuss voter registration in court, they passed a bill in the legislature, signed into law by Governor Fife Symington, doing away with the position of deputy registrar altogether in the state of Arizona, nullifying the court case. When this law went into effect, it became possible for any person to go to a County

Recorder, obtain voter registration forms, and register voters. Why the politicians of the state thought that making it possible for illegal aliens and convicted felons to register voters would be more beneficial to political parties than allowing a few independent voters to be deputy registrars was never explained.

In any event, the new law required a new voter registration form because the signature of a deputy registrar was no longer required to validate a voter registration. Secretary of State Betsey Bayless made up the new voter registration form and sent it to the Justice Department in Washington, D.C., for approval. The new voter registration form had a feature that had an unusual effect on voter registration, one that party politicians did not foresee or even notice for some time. Next to the space marked Party Preference, the Secretary of State had placed a little check box marked None. People registering to vote in Arizona marked that little box so often during the next ten years that Arizona became the state with the highest rate of independent voter registration in the country.

By 1998 there were enough independent voters in the state to pass an initiative for open primary elections. This presented a puzzle for Arizona politicians. It was plain for them to see that they had shot themselves in the foot. This would require a little creative politics.

First, they moved the Presidential Primary election from
September to February, leaving the primary election for state offices in September. Then an opinion was obtained from State Attorney General Janet Napolitano that since the Presidential Primary was not specifically mentioned in the Open Primary legislation, independent voters would not be allowed to vote in the Presidential Primary Election. The other foot came down on independent voters when the Libertarian Party obtained a judgment in Federal District Court to prevent independent voters from voting in the Libertarian Party Primary in Arizona. The Open Primary initiative had in effect been totally nullified. There was no reason why independent voters should not be excluded from voting in the Libertarian Party Primary because the Libertarian Party pays for its own primary election, but federal courts applied this decision also to the public funded major party primaries throughout the United States, effectively excluding independent voters from the provisions of

the Voting Rights Act of 1965.

Party leaders in Arizona had hoped that nullifying the Open Primary would discourage Arizona citizens from registering independent. It seemed to have the opposite effect. Independent voter registration started to go exponential. It was at this point that Republican leaders suddenly discovered that illegal aliens could register to vote. In fact, illegal aliens could register illegal aliens to vote because party politicians had done away with deputy registrars in the early 90's. So Republican leaders drew up an initiative called Proposition 200, which they said would stop illegal aliens from registering to vote and worked the news media and talk radio in Arizona into a state of frenzy. The voters approved Proposition 200. The initiative then went to the legislature, where a Senate bill was drawn up requiring a new voter registration form, the wording of which was taken verbatim from Proposition 200. It was signed into law by Governor Janet Napolitano in April of 2005. But, in fact, it did nothing to stop illegal voter registration except to require voters to show identification at the polls. The only real change in the Arizona voter registration form was removal of the little check box to be checked by persons registering as independent voters.

So, once again, the Secretary of State of Arizona sent a voter registration form to the Justice Department in Washington, D. C., to be approved, and the new voter registration form went into effect in September of 2005. In November of the same year a Republican Party spokesman in Pinal County, Arizona, spilled the beans about the real reason for Proposition 200.

> "In the 2004 gubernatorial election, Democrat candidates were required to obtain 4,037 signatures, while Republicans had to collect 4,603 to earn a spot on the ballot. Independents, however, were forced to collect more than three times as many signatures—a whopping 14,694—to make the ballot.

> "The numbers are based on a percentage of registered voters statewide. Independents account for nearly 25% of all voters, a number that's up seven percent since 2000 and continually increasing.

> "However, Bill Bridwell, President of the Western Pinal Republican Club, feels

that increase is misleading and is the result of a voter registration form created by former Secretary of State Betsey Bayless. The form had a box for voters to check for no party preference. If they wanted to register as Republicans or Democrats, they had to actually fill in a blank.

"'The independent growth trend, in my opinion, is not as large as it would appear......This huge growth of the independent voters occurred from the time that voter registration form was issued until three months ago when a new form was created. We are finding they are now declaring themselves to be Democrat or Republican. It's likely those numbers aren't going to continue to grow like they had for the previous three or four years.'

"Bridwell also feels independent voters don't play a significant role in Arizona politics.

"'While there's a large block of independent voters, they haven't shown up in the polls. It still is as it always has been, a two party system in Arizona. If you are not a major party candidate, there is no large block of voters that will turn out for you.....If they were significant they would have had an impact in the last two election cycles. When you look at the numbers, they just aren't there.'"

Mr. Bridwell was not just making an idle boast. Independent voter registration in Arizona did decrease.

2000-2002	107,715
2002-2004	165,771
2004-2006	26,384

If independent voter registration had decreased to 0, it might have meant something. As it was, independent voter registration decreased from 80,000 per year to 13,000 per year and then began to rise again as Arizona citizens learned that they could still register as independent voters. By 2008 it was back up to about 40,000 per year. Political parties in Arizona had done their best and accomplished nothing. At the present time, while independent voter registration continues to increase, the news media reports that voter registration for both major parties is decreasing in Arizona.

Chapter 14

It is not to be expected that political parties and their corrupt politicians are going to see the error of their ways and suddenly repent of the evil they have done. They are going to see the error of their ways and attempt to stay in power. They are going to use every unfair advantage, every dishonest practice, every form of untruth, all of the public revenues they can lay their hands on, and all of the power of public administration to try to stay where they are.

Independent voters, having arrived at the point they now occupy, have to be realistic about their government. It is controlled by self-created societies. There are a couple of ways to weaken what George Washington called the "artificial authority" of political parties. The first is voter registration. Independent voters are already doing well in this capacity just by registering to vote, much better than political parties. Americans by instinct are abandoning the European agendas of political parties. This by itself would eventually bring down the two-party system in the

United States.

What is needed is something to speed the process. It could take a long time for this to happen by nature. Without independent candidates for office, the process will be very slow. Who wants to be an independent candidate?

Eccentric billionaire Ross Perot was an independent candidate for President. Former Democratic Vice-Presidential candidate Joe Lieberman won re-election to his Senate seat as an independent candidate after losing his party primary election. Ralph Nader sometimes runs as a Green Party candidate and sometimes as an independent candidate. Bernie Sanders is a Socialist Party member who runs as an independent candidate to be elected to Congress. That is fine. Anyone can run as an independent candidate, including party members. Party members can be considered to be Americans who have subjected their independence to the control of parties, but who are still free to exercise independence when they choose to do so.

The problem at the present time is that almost all candidates who run as independent candidates are really maverick party candidates who have spilled over from two-party politics. You see very few actual independent voters registering as candidates. There are two reasons why all independent voters should consider registering as candidates. The first is voter registration, as I have mentioned. Candidates for public office can obtain some sort of capacity for registering voters, whatever state they are running in. If the goal is to win a voter registration race, then independent candidates are the catalyst that will speed the process.

Secondly, if George Washington was right, which he was, then all candidates for public office should be independent candidates. That means that political party candidates have a bad effect on American government, and independent candidates have a good effect no matter how many Democrats think that Ralph Nader caused Al Gore to lose the 2000 Presidential election. The truth of the matter is that Ralph Nader, Joe Lieberman, Bernie Sanders, and Ross Perot were all political party candidates running in independent candidacies, just as Aaron Burr did before killing Alexander Hamilton. A true independent candidate would say that independent candidacy is the correct way to run for public office, while political party candidacies are an incorrect way.

Political party candidates really represent the extremes of European politics. Ralph Nader represents a German political party even when he is running as an independent candidate. The major party candidates who win their party primaries represent European socialism and European nationalism as it is being applied to the United States. These people do nothing after being elected to office except what they see done in European governments by European political party politicians. At the present time we see American political parties giving public revenues to American banks and businesses, which was what was done in Europe when the economic crisis hit in 2008. We see a takeover of American businesses by the government and an attempt to socialize American medicine. None of these ideas originated in the United States.

In the European Union today there are only some political parties recognized as having the right to participate. The two major parties in the United States carry that attitude into American politics, moving in state governments from time to time to eradicate minor parties, such as Arizona Attorney General Terry Goddard's elimination of most small political parties in

Arizona a few years ago, leaving only the two major parties and the Libertarians as recognized political parties in the state. The two major parties represent European elitism in its most virulent form.

The two major parties today believe that voters are the property of the two major political parties. Both major parties are now pro-slavery with political parties as the only ones having the right to own slaves. But the main problem that they have is that now all problems that need to be solved by government are solved by the same means that political parties used to solve the problem of slavery. All serious problems are turned over to the Supreme Court, the branch of government that could not tell that kidnapping of people from their homes in Africa was a crime, resolved in the same manner that the Supreme Court resolved slavery, (one political party always takes the wrong side of any question before the court, usually the party with the most power), and then Congress needs to increase taxes so that members of Congress and other government officials can be paid more. Then there needs to be a bailout of banks and big businesses so that the economy can be stimulated. As Americans learned in the 1770's, honest government under political parties does not come without a price.

The way for Americans to break out of this stranglehold is for ordinary Americans to register as independent candidates for office, especially for state and local offices, where they have the best chance of being elected. In doing this, Americans have to be realistic. Most voters in the United States are still party members. Party members vote for party candidates. That is what they are trained to do. They practice year around in gambling casinos and other places where there are games of chance. The goal of the political party voter is to vote for the winning candidate. Many of the voters who are registered as independent voters are, in fact, political party voters. We need to respect the right of all Americans to vote the way they choose to vote.

It is unlikely that any independent voter at the present time is going to register as a candidate, become known to the voters by unbiased coverage in the news media, and be elected on election day. Party controlled elections do not work that way. First of all, party politicians take unimaginable amounts of money from public revenues and give it directly to the news media in return for exclusive coverage of political party candidates. That is the way the system works. The public is unlikely to ever know that an independent candidate is running for office. Secondly, the nomination petition requirements for independent candidates in many states are far beyond the capacity of most Americans to meet.

Go register as a candidate and start getting signatures anyway. Candidates for office have the capacity to register voters. An independent candidate at this time needs to be registering voters, not worrying about getting elected. Independent voters have to look at the realities.

Suppose a college student registers as an independent candidate for the state legislature. In Arizona that candidate could then go to a county recorder and obtain two hundred voter registration forms. So could anyone else, but why would anyone else do it?

Then the student sets up a table on his college campus and says to each student passing by, "Hey, how about signing my nomination petition.?"

An independent candidate in Arizona has to get about four times as many signatures to get on the ballot as a major party candidate, but it is within reach for a state office.

About three out of four students will say, "Sorry, not registered to vote."

Even a political science student could figure out what to do with the two hundred voter registration forms after a while. Once the two hundred forms are gone, the County Recorder will give the candidate another two hundred.

College campuses are the best places to register voters because most college students are not registered to vote, and they are more likely to register independent than anyone else. If independent voters are smart, they will not emulate political party voter registration. When I first registered to vote in Arizona, I had to sit through a lecture by the deputy registrar about how Arizona had a closed primary, and an independent voter could not vote in the primary election. The best way to register voters is to register them the way they say they want to register. Given current trends, there will be more independent voters than Democrats or Republicans.

The reason why independent voters need to start

registering voters is because political parties are so incapable at this particular thing. Even with the wide open voter registration Arizona now has, voter registration has gone up less than 10% from 48% in 1988. The reason for the slight increase is that it is much easier to register to vote now.

Chapter 15

The kind of government we have depends on two things, registered voters and candidates for office, two things that political parties try to eliminate and limit in government, leaving only their corrupt candidates to be approved by party voters. Party controlled elections are not free and open elections, the kind of elections required by the Constitutions of most states. We will know we are having free and open elections in the United States when independent candidates are running against independent candidates and being elected.

Obviously, that is going to take some amount of time, since there are but few independent voters running as candidates for office at the present time. , and if there are any, the news media makes certain that the voters do not know anything about them.

So what political views should independent candidates represent?

An independent voter is a United States citizen registered to vote. United States citizens are allowed to have whatever political beliefs they want to have. Political parties are organizations with party platforms, agendas, and regimentation. They do not want independent voters voting in their primary elections because they regard themselves as private clubs. However, they are in favor of independent voters paying for the elections that their private clubs hold. This makes them different from other private clubs.

With a news media paid to give party candidates exclusive promotion in the news, voters have no idea what individual independent candidates stand for. That is an obstacle that will have to be overcome. Right now individual independent voters just need to register as candidates for public office, whatever their personal beliefs or political philosophies. They need to do it in order to register voters, not with the expectation to immediately be elected to office. If enough independent voters register as candidates, some will be elected.

Maybe we can get some of the unemployed, homeless people who were put out of their houses by the economic crisis to register as candidates. Just think of it as a job application. If you are not elected, it would probably not be the first time you were rejected. But if you register a few voters, then you have performed a valuable service for your country instead of just being idle the way the political parties have you.

If independent voters take this attitude toward government, they will break the power of the two major parties fairly rapidly because there will be a great contrast between political party candidates and independent candidates. Independent candidates can be ordinary Americans, who register as candidates, solicit no money from the voters, make no expenditures, seek no publicity, and who improve the government by registering voters. Speaking for myself, if I went to the polls on election day and saw two major party candidates and an independent candidate on the ballot for an office, I would vote for the independent candidate sight unseen just because I do not like political party candidates.

Now suppose that there were enough voters like me to completely replace the people now in Congress. Then suppose that we discover that these independent candidates we have elected are all dishonest people. We will have a better government than we now have because they would not know how to steal money as fast as the Congressional incumbents we have. You do not work up to trillion dollar bailouts overnight.

I also do not like the news media because they make no secret of the fact that they are there to discourage independent voters and independent candidates for office. When independent deputy registrars were dismissed in Arizona in 1988, I went to the office of a major newspaper, talked with a reporter for about an hour, returned home, and then received a phone call from the reporter. He was calling to tell me that his editor was not going to allow him to write the story. The same situation arose when I sent the article from a local newspaper to major news outlets showing that the two major parties had conspired to decrease independent voter registration in Arizona. It was a story they refused to cover. Independent voters and independent candidates should expect this kind of treatment from the news media.

Secondly, if the news media does talk to an independent candidate, they will take one of two attitudes: 1. It is extremely humorous that you would try to run for office as an independent candidate. 2. You have done something terribly wrong in trying to run for office as an independent candidate. The best way to deal with the news media as an independent is to expect nothing good from them. We independent voters believe in freedom of the press. If the news media wants to become irrelevant, they should be allowed to become irrelevant.

Finally, we have no argument with political parties. We just don't like their form of government. What we are going to do as individual independent voters is to use what remains of our individual rights as United States citizens to participate in government. If political parties do not like it, they will continue to do what they have always done. What is there to argue about?

It seems to me that political parties are in a perfect position to show the world how good political party government can be. They control elections. They control the news media. They control all public offices. They control the people. So what is the matter, political parties?

Could it be that President George Washington was right in what he said about political parties.

The Nazi Party did not provide Germany with

good government. The Communist Party did not provide Russia with good government. The Fascist Party did not provide Italy with good government. The claim of American and British parties is that if there are two parties instead of one, then it is good government. So each party tries to eliminate the other party. The only thing they seem to agree on is that independent voters should not be allowed to participate in government.

Sorry, there are too many independent voters to run that game now. We will see you at the polls on general election day. My prediction is that political parties in the United States will continue to decline. I do not see that as a bad thing. Anyone in the United States can register as an independent voter. The reason they can do that is because when the United States began, all voters were independent voters. The parties may try to stop independent voter registration in other states the way they did in Arizona. It will not be successful. Independent voters all over the United States know what was done in Arizona and are watching for similar actions by political parties in other states. Independent voters all over the United States are seeking ballot access in the courts. That is a good thing, but will have limited success as long as political parties are appointing judges.

The best thing independent voters can do is to start registering as candidates for office by whatever means is available to them in party controlled elections, especially for state and local offices. They should also seek appointment as election officials. In Arizona independent voters can be election officials, but according to present laws, supervisors of election officials have to be party members. Independent voters need to start registering voters in order to protect their right to register and to vote. There will not be much to vote for in the near future because of the two major parties, but that can be improved over time by the existence of independent candidates.

What I have predicted is going to happen in any event, so we might as well just go ahead and do it. Political parties are too incompetent at government to keep up with the needs of the people, just as they were with the question of slavery. The difference now is that independent voters can keep the two major parties from putting together a Civil War. Here in the United States, the people are the government. Any time they are complaining about the government, they are complaining about themselves. If they support political parties, they are going to have bad government. I say register people to vote and let them decide what kind of government they are going to have.

Political parties have proven their limited ability to register voters. People do not really want to vote for corrupt government. Some nations combat this deficiency by requiring people to register to vote. That does not seem to help much. The people still do not get enthusiastic about corrupt political parties. In the United States, independent voters, having achieved a higher rate of voter registration than political parties for the first time since 1800, are going to increase until they control the government. The goals of independent voters will not be specific party contentions, but will be to improve elections in the United States because they are now finding that they do not have the same opportunities in government that party politicians have secured to themselves. There will be a de-Europeanization of American politics at the same time parties are trying to enforce European political party interpretation of government.

It all hinges on voter registration. As an independent voter, I encourage all Americans who are eligible to register to vote. That includes Americans who want to belong to self-created societies.

Chapter 16

In the final analysis, independent voters will succeed in American politics while political parties will fail because of the same reasons the United States engaged in a war of revolution against Great Britain in the first place. Political parties are too expensive and too inefficient to be sustained in government. We might compare the success of the two-party system in the United States with Napoleon's invasion of Russia.

There has been little opposition to party control since the election of 1800, when a political party came into power in American politics. In like manner, after a stern warning to Napoleon from Russian Czar Alexander, the Russians were almost completely ineffective against the French army of a half million soldiers until the battle of Borodino, in which the French lost a substantial number of soldiers in removing the last obstacle to the capture of Moscow.

 But it was a hollow victory. Most of the inhabitants of Moscow had abandoned their city, and the departing government had set it on fire. There was nothing there to sustain the French army, and as winter began to set in, Napoleon had no choice but to retreat the way he had come. Of his half million army, only 20,000 lived to escape their invasion of Russia.

The difference between the two-party system in the United States and the Grand Armee is that American political party members will not have to die, but will come out of their defeat better off than they were under party control. Except for the engagement at Borodino, the Russian army did not directly confront the French army and did not have as much effect on its defeat as the disease, starvation, and Russian winter into which the great leader of the French army had led his troops.

As we now approach another party controlled election in 2012, I say that the two major parties are about where Napoleon was before the battle of Borodino. They are going to fight the voters to gain control of the government one last time. Then they are going to retreat.

Here is why political parties are done. They have borrowed too much money. The United States has been out of debt one time in its history. That was during the Presidency of Andrew Jackson. Although I may have berated President Jackson for starting the Democratic

Party, he is to be commended for his handling of government finances during his administration. He beat down the banks and got the government out of debt. However, a year into the administration of Martin van Buren, Jackson's successor in the Presidency, the Panic of 1837 put the national economy into a recession similar to the one we are in now. The government went into debt again, increasing the money borrowed each administration thereafter to its present level of sixteen trillion dollars. The national debt is the Russian winter that will bring down the two-party system.

When I was growing up during the fifties and sixties, the national debt was a great concern to party leaders. There were spokesmen in both parties who warned against getting further into debt. But there was an arms race going on. World Communism had to be opposed. Poverty had to be stopped in the United States. Government expenditures could not be brought down overnight.

The amount of debt back then seems insignificant compared to the obstacle it is now. But the problem was the same then as it is now. Political parties of today cannot function without increasing the debt.

That means that the government of the United States cannot function without increasing the debt as long as political parties control the government. The mistake back then was not the intent of the American people. They intended to pay the debt. Their mistake was in believing that there was a way to reduce and pay the debt through party politics.

Forget paying the debt through political parties. They are only going to increase the debt. After reaching the astronomical figure of five trillion dollars in the 1990's, the Republican administration of George W. Bush increased the debt another five trillion dollars to finance two wars during his eight years in office. All of that money expended did not help the national economy. The nation fell into financial disaster as Bush left office. The rate of borrowing increased even more with the Democratic Party administration of Barack Obama. The Obama administration has increased the debt by another five trillion dollars in three and a half years time.

Where do we go from here?

It is surely a time for panic, for increased party contentions, for blame and for finger pointing. I am sure we will see plenty of these things before political parties are done with what they are doing.   It is the nature of party politics.

We need to go a different direction. During the first term of President Bill Clinton, the issue of the national debt came to the forefront of party politics. Republicans in Congress, who had control of the legislature, balked at raising the debt ceiling during the term of a Democratic President.   The President responded by announcing that he was shutting down the government. It was during this face off between the President and Republican members of Congress that, after listening to a speech by the President, I signed my income tax return check, which I had just received, and sent it to President Clinton along with a letter requesting that it be applied toward payment of the national debt.

About a week later the check was returned along with a letter from someone on the White House staff explaining that the President could not accept my donation.

That's odd, I thought. I am sure he would have accepted the money if I had said I was donating it to his re-election campaign.

So I started sending the check to various members of Congress, explaining what had happened when I sent it to the President and asking how the money could be applied toward payment of the debt. Same result.

After several tries, I sent the check to a Representative from Arizona named Sam Coppersmith who styled himself as a Jacksonian Democrat. He seemed to have some of Jackson's knowledge of government finances because he wrote to inform me that he had forwarded my donation to the Bureau of the Public Debt, and he was grateful for my contribution. Since that time I have tried to contribute a small donation each year to this worthy cause, also known as the United States of America. Each time I contribute I get a little letter in return thanking me and stating that three million and some odd dollars were contributed during the previous year.

So Americans do have a way to pay the debt. I would encourage all Americans, not just independent voters, to make a small contribution from time to time to this cause. My political party friends do not see the logic in doing this.

You should send three dollars to the Obama campaign, they say. Then you would have a chance of having dinner with George Clooney.

Or, if you really wanted to help America, you would send the money to Mitt Romney's campaign.

No, I really think I would rather send it to the Bureau of the Public Debt. Then I can say that independent voters are trying to pay the debt, while political parties and their politicians are trying to increase it. I am like a Russian partisan harassing Napoleon's huge army as it started from Moscow back to France. I don't have to do much to win this war. Whether many other independent voters join me in this kind of direct attack on party excesses, I am going to come out on top because independent voters do not benefit in any way from the money borrowed by political party politicians to finance their political party projects, and it will only take a seven percentage point increase in the number of independent voters nationwide before they will outnumber all political party members in the United States.

Independent voters are not as excitable and panicky as party members. What we do is just find the right direction and go that way.

Bibliography

A Short History of England, Edward P. Cheney, 1918, The Athenaeum Press, Ginn and Company, Boston, U.S.A.

The Constitution of the United States

George Washington's Farewell Address

Wikepedia Encyclopedia

The Maricopa Monitor Newspaper, Maricopa, Arizona

State of Arizona Registration Report, Arizona Secretary of State

www.ingramcontent.com/pod-product-compliance
Lightning Source LLC
Chambersburg PA
CBHW072313290526
45794CB00002B/642